A PARRAGON BOOK

Published by Parragon Book Service Ltd,
Units 13-17, Avonbridge Trading Estate, Atlantic Road,
Avonmouth, Bristol BS11 9QD

Produced by The Templar Company plc,
Pippbrook Mill, London Road, Dorking,
Surrey RH4 1JE

Written by Robert Snedden
Series Editor Robert Snedden
Designed by Mark Summersby

Printed and bound in the UK

ISBN 0 7525 1682 5

FACTFINDERS

CARD
GAMES

• PARRAGON •

TITLES IN THIS SERIES INCLUDE:

ASTRONOMY

CARD GAMES

CLANS & TARTANS

FASTEST CARS

FLAGS OF THE WORLD

HANDGUNS & SMALL ARMS

HISTORIC BRITAIN

HUMAN BODY

INVENTIONS

NATURAL DISASTERS

CONTENTS

INTRODUCTION

Card games are a wonderful form of entertainment. A pack of cards is portable, requires no power source and can be used just about anywhere.

There are hundreds of different games that can be played with a pack or two of cards. In their demands on the players they range from a very simple game, such as Snap, which can be shared and enjoyed by adults and very young children, to a game such as Contract Bridge (not described here) that requires a great deal of thought and strategy and may be played seriously at competition level.

This book doesn't spend too much time with serious card games. Although card games can be, and frequently are, played for money, a lot of entertainment can be had by substituting counters or matches for coins. Games, such as Poker, that lose much of their spice when not played for meaningful stakes, are not included in the present book. The emphasis here is on family fun. There are games here to while away an idle moment or two, whether in the company of one person or several. There are even a few games to play when you are on your own.

Card games can be educational too. Children can get practise with counting and number order by

playing cards – Casino is a particularly good game for teaching young children basic counting skills. Children can also learn to recognise patterns and acquire memory skills by playing a game such as Rummy. Perhaps most importantly, they can learn social skills, such as how to win and lose graciously, by playing on equal terms with adults. The child who sits down to play a game with his or her parents feels part of the family.

In the following pages you will find a selection of popular card games that will provide relaxing diversions when you don't want to think too hard, or mental challenges and stimulation if you want them.

There are card games to suit every member of the family here. Some of them you may recognise, while others may be new to you. Some games you may know under different names or slightly different rules. If you want to amend the rules of a game to suit you and your family and friends that is quite all right. Local variations are common in card games. Just be sure that all the players are playing to the same rules before the game starts! The important thing is for everyone to enjoy playing. Have fun!

BEGGAR MY NEIGHBOUR

THIS GAME IS PARTICULARLY SUITABLE FOR YOUNG PLAYERS

All the cards are dealt out to the players - it doesn't matter if some have more cards than others. The players put their cards in a pile face down in front of them without looking at them.

The player on the dealer's left turns up his top card and puts it in the centre of the table. The next player does the same and so on round the table. If one player turns up an Ace, King, Queen or Jack the next player has to pay four cards for an Ace, three for a King, two for a Queen and one for a Jack. These are played on top of the central pile.

If the player turns up another Ace, King, Queen or Jack while he is paying he stops and the next player has to pay him the correct number of cards. When a pay-off is completed the winner picks up all of the cards in the middle and puts them face down at the bottom of the pile in front of him.

If a player runs out of cards he drops out of the game. The winner is the player who collects all 52 cards.

BLACK MARIA

THREE PLAYERS (UP TO SEVEN IS POSSIBLE)

The object of the game is to avoid taking tricks containing the Ace, King and Queen of Spades or any of the Hearts.

Remove the 2♣ from the pack and deal out all the cards. (If more than four play the 2♠, 2♦, and 3♣ may be removed as necessary to ensure that each player gets the same number of cards.)

Each player begins by passing three cards face down to the player on his right. If there are more than four players only two cards are passed.

The player to the left of the dealer leads for the first trick. The other players must follow suit if possible and the trick is taken by the highest card of the suit led. There are no trumps. A player who does not hold any cards of the suit led may play a card of another suit or use the opportunity to get rid of any penalty cards held.

At the end of play each player counts up the number of penalty points he has taken in tricks as follows:

EACH HEART	**1 POINT**
ACE OF SPADES	**7 POINTS**
KING OF SPADES	**10 POINTS**
QUEEN OF SPADES	**13 POINTS**

If a player takes all the penalty cards he is awarded 43 penalty points.

The winner is the player with fewest points after an agreed number of deals.

CASINO

TWO PLAYERS

Deal four cards to each player and four, face-up, on the table to form the lay-out.

The object is to score points by

TAKING MOST CARDS	**3 POINTS**
FOR BIG CASINO (10♦)	**2 POINTS**
FOR LITTLE CASINO (2♦)	**1 POINT**
FOR TAKING MOST SPADES	**1 POINT**
FOR EACH ACE CAPTURED	**1 POINT**
FOR EACH SWEEP MADE	**1 POINT**

The non-dealer begins the play. There are five things he can do:

1. He may pair one of his cards with one or more cards of the same rank in the layout. For example a King can be used to capture any Kings in the layout.

LAYOUT

15

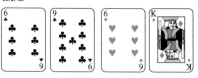

The K♦ may be paired with both the K♠ and the K♥

2. He may capture one or more cards in the layout which have a pip total that adds up to the same number as one of the cards he holds in his hand. For example, if he holds a 9 he may capture a 6 and 3, a 5 and 4, or any other combinations of cards adding up to a total of 9.

It would be possible to capture all four cards in the layout at once if, as in the example below, a 6, 3, 2 and 7 were showing. If all four cards are taken at once this is termed a sweep and is worth one point.

LAYOUT

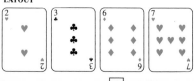

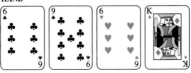

All four cards in the layout may be captured with the 9♣

3. If he holds a pair in his hand he may play one to a card of the same rank on the layout announcing, 'Building 4s' (or 5s, or 10s, according to the rank of the card). The aim is to capture all three cards in the next turn with the remaining card of the pair.

LAYOUT

HAND

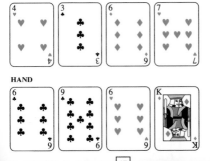

17

The 6♣ is played to the 6♦ in the layout. Both may be captured with the 6♥ on the player's next turn.

4. He can build a total on the layout that he can capture on his next turn,. For example, he may add a 4 from his hand to an Ace and 3 on the layout, announcing 'Building 8', with the intention of capturing all of the cards with an 8 in his next turn.

LAYOUT

HAND

The player announces 'Building 9' and adds a 6 to the 3♣. The build can then be captured with the 9♣ on the player's next turn.

5. If he can do none of the above he must trail by adding one of his cards to the layout.

The second player may, if he can, add to a build on the table, thereby possibly preventing the first player from capturing it, but only if he himself holds a capturing card. For example, if there is a build of 6 on the table (a 2 and a 4, say), the second player may add a 3, saying 'Building 9', provided he holds a 9 in his hand with which to capture the build on the next turn. No build may count more than ten.

A build counts as a single card and individual cards in the build may not be captured by pairing.

The second player may, if he wishes, begin another build on the layout. A player who makes or adds to a build in one turn must either capture or add to it on the next.

When all the cards in the players' hands have been played out another deal is made and the game continues until all the cards in the pack have been dealt.

The game ends when all the cards have been played. Any cards remaining in the layout are taken by the player who won the last trick. This is not awarded a point for a sweep, however. The players now sort through the cards they have won and total their scores. The game may continue until one player has reached an agreed score, say 11 or 21.

CATCH THE TEN

36 CARD PACK (REMOVE 5S, 4S, 3S AND 2S FROM THE STANDARD PACK)

TWO TO EIGHT PLAYERS (FOUR, PLAYING IN PARTNERSHIPS, IS BEST)

All players must have the same number of cards. If five or seven play remove the 6♠ from the pack, if eight play either remove all four 6s or add the 5s.

The object of the game is to win tricks, particularly those that capture the five top trump cards.

Deal out all the cards one at a time. The dealer exposes the last card to determine the trump suit for the hand.

The player to the left of the dealer leads for the first trick. The winner of each trick takes the lead for the next. Players must follow suit if possible and the trick is won by the highest card of the suit led or the highest trump played. Ace ranks high.

After the hand has been played out scores are added up as follows:

TRUMP JACK	**11 POINTS**
TRUMP ACE	**4 POINTS**
TRUMP KING	**3 POINTS**

| **TRUMP QUEEN** | **2 POINTS** |
| **TRUMP TEN** | **10 POINTS** |

In addition, each side, or player if playing singly, gets one point for every card held in tricks above those originally dealt. For example, if a side took six tricks it would score 6 points for the six cards won over the eighteen they had to begin with. The winner is the first to 41 points.

CHEAT

THREE TO SIX PLAYERS

A GOOD CHILDREN'S GAME

Deal out all the cards. It doesn't matter if some players get more than others. The first player takes one, two, three or four cards from his hand and lays them face down on the table, saying 'Aces'. The next player does the same, this time saying 'Twos'. Play continues around the table in this way up to 'Kings'.

At any time anyone may challenge an announcement by calling 'Cheat!' The cards that have just been played are then turned face up. If they are not what they were claimed to be, the person who played them must pick up all the cards played so far and add them to his hand. If the cards are what the player said they were the challenger must pick up all the cards. Play then continues with whoever won the challenge. The object is to be the first to run out of cards.

CRIBBAGE

TWO PLAYERS

CRIBBAGE BOARD TO KEEP SCORE

The object is to score 121 points over as many deals as
are necessary. Cards rank according to their face value
with Ace counting 1 and court cards counting 10. Scores
are best kept by moving pegs around a cribbage board
(called 'pegging').

The cards are cut for deal. The player cutting the lowest
card deals first. Six cards are dealt to each player.

After examining his cards each player puts two cards face
down on the table to form a 'crib' of four cards. The crib
will eventually be scored by the dealer but is not looked
at yet. In playing cards to the crib the players will be aim-
ing to keep four cards in their hands that have good scoring combinations. At the same time the dealer will hope
to play advantageous cards to his crib.

SCORING COMBINATIONS:

FIFTEEN (2 POINTS) - ANY COMBINATION OF TWO OR MORE CARDS TOTALLING 15 IN FACE VALUE.

PAIR (2 POINTS) - TWO CARDS OF THE SAME RANK

PRIAL OR PAIR ROYAL (6 POINTS) - THREE CARDS OF THE SAME RANK

DOUBLE PAIR ROYAL (12 POINTS) - FOUR CARDS OF THE SAME RANK

RUN (1 POINT PER CARD) - THREE OR MORE CARDS IN ORDER OF RANK

FLUSH (1 POINT PER CARD) - FOUR CARDS OF THE SAME SUIT IN ONE HAND

A straight run, i.e. with all cards in the same suit, counts as both a run and a flush.

The non-dealer lifts the top half of the undealt pack and the dealer removes the top card of the bottom half and places it face up on top of the pack as the 'starter'. If it is a Jack the dealer pegs 2 points 'for his heels'.

Beginning with the non-dealer, each player in turn plays a card face up in front of him, announcing the total value of cards played by both so far. A player bringing the total to exactly 15 pegs 2 points. The score must not exceed 31. If a player cannot play without taking the score over this he says 'Go'. The other player adds as many cards as possible without exceeding 31 and pegs 1 point for go and 2 points if he makes the score 31 exactly. If any cards remain in hand the cards played so far are turned face down and play begins again with the cards remaining. If one player runs out of cards the other continues alone.

Points are also pegged for runs and pairs made during play. For example, Player One plays 4, Player Two plays 6, Player One plays 5 and pegs 3 for a run of three. If Player Two can then play either a 3 or a 7 he will peg 4 for a run of four. Or if Player One plays a 7 and Player Two plays another 7 he pegs 2 for a pair; if Player One can play a third 7 he pegs 6 for a pair royal.

After the play is over the show begins. Each player, beginning with the non-dealer, spreads the four cards in his hand face up on the table. In combination with the starter these make a five-card hand which he then scores for any of the combinations listed above. Any given card may be used in more than one combination and may be used more than once in the same combination, provided at least one of the other cards in the combination changes. A flush can count 5 points if the starter card is in the same suit as all four cards held. A player holding the Jack of the same suit as the starter also pegs 1 'for his nob'.

After reckoning his hand the dealer also counts the score in the crib and adds it to his total. Only five-card flushes count when totalling the crib.

Play ends the moment a player 'pegs out' by reaching the target of 121.

EXAMPLE HAND

CARDS HELD:

STARTER CARD:

SCORING COMBINATIONS
4 for 15 (7♥ 8♥, 7♥ 8♠)
4 for the two pairs (6s and 8s)
12 for four runs of three(6♥ 7♥ 8♥, 6♥ 7♥ 8♠, 6♠ 7♥ 8♥,
6♠ 7♥ 8♠)

For a total score of 20.

DOMINOES

THREE TO EIGHT PLAYERS

EACH PLAYER SHOULD HAVE A STOCK OF MATCHSTICKS, COUNTERS OR SIMILAR

Before the deal each player adds one matchstick, counter or whatever to a central kitty. The cards are then dealt out as far as they will go, it doesn't matter if everyone doesn't have the same number.

The player who has the 7♦ begins the play. The player on his left has the choice of playing the 6♦ below the 7, the 8♦ above the 7 or another 7. If he cannot make any of these plays he must add one unit to the kitty and play passes to the next player.

Play continues around the table with sequences being built up to the Kings and down to the Aces from the 7s. Whenever a player is unable to add to a sequence he adds another unit to the kitty.

The winner is the first to get rid of his last card. He takes the kitty.

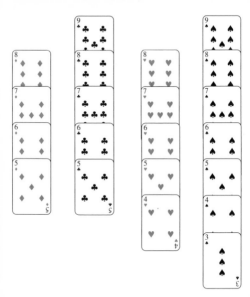

The player going next has the option of playing one of the following: 4♦ 9♦, 4♣ 10♣, 3♥ 9♥, or 2♠ 10♠.

GERMAN WHIST

TWO PLAYERS

Deal 13 cards to each player. Place the remainder of the pack face down on the table and turn the top card up to determine trumps for the game. Ace ranks high.

The non-dealer leads first. The other player must follow suit if he can, or, if unable to, he may win the trick by playing a trump card or elect to lose it by playing a card of another suit. The winner of the trick takes the upturned top card and the other player takes the face-down card beneath it without showing it to his opponent. The next card in the pile is then turned face up. The winner of the trick leads for the next one.

When the pack has been exhausted the players play out the cards in their hands. The winner is the one who takes the most tricks.

GIN RUMMY

PAPER AND PENCIL TO KEEP SCORES

The players cut for deal, lowest card dealing first. Ten cards are dealt to each player. The next card is turned face up on the table to start the discard pile, the rest are placed face down beside it.

The object of the game is to be the first to 'knock' by laying down all or most of the cards held in sets or melds. A set is three or four cards of the same rank or a sequence of three or more cards in the same suit.

A player may knock only if the total value of the unmelded cards in his hand is 10 or less. (Aces count 1, court cards 10, others cards face value). A hand in which all ten cards are melded is 'gin'.

The non-dealer may begin by taking the face-up card in exchange for a card in his hand. If he declines to do so the option of taking the face-up card passes to the dealer. If the dealer does not want the face-up card the non-dealer takes the top card from the stockpile. If he keeps it he must throw one of his cards on the discard pile. Each player in turn then either takes the top discard or the top stockpile card and plays one card to the discard pile.

The hand continues until one player knocks by making one final discard and then spreading his cards face up on the table, divided into melds and 'deadwood' (unmelded cards). The other player then melds whichever cards he can and lays off any unmelded cards to his opponent's hand by adding to sets and sequences if possible. He may not lay off if the other player has gone 'gin'.

EXAMPLE OF A 'GIN' HAND

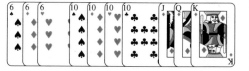

OPPONENT'S HAND

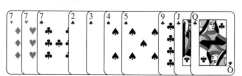

DEADWOOD SCORE: 29
KNOCKER SCORES 29 + 25 = 54 POINTS

The player who has knocked scores the difference between his opponent's deadwood score and his own. A gin gets the opponent's deadwood score plus a bonus of 25 points. However, if the opponent's score is equal to or less than the knocker's score then the knocker is 'undercut'. In this case the opponent scores the difference in deadwood scores plus a bonus of 25 points.

Each player deals in turn and the winner is the first to 100 points. Both players then add 25 points for each hand won and the winner gets an additional 100 points for the game. As many games may be played as desired.

GO FISH!

TWO TO FIVE PLAYERS

THIS GAME IS SUITABLE FOR YOUNG PLAYERS.

The object of the game is to be the first to get rid of all
your cards by laying them down in sets of four of a kind,
e.g. four Kings, four 3s and so on.

If there are two or three players deal seven cards to each,
if more deal five cards each. The remainder are placed
face down on the table as the fish pile.

The player on the dealer's left begins. Addressing one of
the other players he says, 'Mark' (or whoever) 'give me
your 7s.' The player must have at least one of the rank of
cards he is asking for in his hand. If Mark has any of the
cards asked for he must pass them over. The asker can
continue to ask for cards of any rank from any player,
provided that he holds at least one card of that rank himself, until a player does not have the cards asked for. If a
player does not have the cards asked for he says 'Go
fish!' The asking player takes a card from the fish pile
and his turn ends. The person who said 'Go fish!' then
becomes the asker.

As soon as a player succeeds in collecting all four cards in
a set he places them face down in front of him. The winner is the first player to set down all of his cards.

KNOCKOUT WHIST

TWO TO SEVEN PLAYERS

Deal seven cards to each player and turn up the next card to determine trumps. The dealer leads for the first trick. The winner of each trick takes the lead for the next. Players must follow suit if possible and the trick is won by the highest card of the suit led or the highest trump played. Ace ranks high.

Anyone who fails to take a trick is knocked out of the game. The player who won the most tricks in the hand shuffles the cards and deals six to each player. After examining his hand, he announces what trumps will be for this round and leads for the first trick. If two or more players win the same number of tricks they may cut the cards to determine who makes the next deal.

Play continues with the number of cards being dealt reduced by one on each round. The winner is the last player left when everyone else has been knocked out after failing to take a trick. On the seventh round only one card is dealt and the winner of the game will be the winner of this single trick.

LINGER LONGER

THREE PLAYERS (UP TO SIX IS POSSIBLE)

The object of the game is to be the last player holding
any cards.

Deal ten cards to each player (if four are playing deal
seven cards, if five deal six, if six deal five). Turn up the
next card in the pack to determine trumps and place the
rest face down on the table to form the stockpile.

The player to the left of the dealer leads for the first
trick. The winner of each trick takes the lead for the next.
Players must follow suit if possible and the trick is won
by the highest card of the suit led or the highest trump
played. Ace ranks high.

Tricks themselves are not scored. However, the winner of
a trick takes a card from the stockpile into his hand
before leading for the next trick. If a player uses up all
the cards in his hand he must drop out of play. The winner will be the last player left with any cards in his hand.

If the stockpile is used up before there is a winner all of
the tricks are shuffled together to form a new stockpile.

MATRIMONY

THREE TO TEN PLAYERS

**EACH PLAYER SHOULD HAVE THE SAME NUMBER OF
MATCHSTICKS, COUNTERS OR SIMILAR**

A large sheet of paper marked with five compartments
labelled Matrimony, Intrigue, Confederacy, Pair and Best
is needed for the layout. Alternatively, five saucers
labelled in the same way could be used.

The dealer distributes any number of counters he
chooses between the five compartments – each should
have at least two. Each player then takes from his own
stock one counter less than the number chosen by the
dealer and distributes them as he pleases.

The cards are shuffled and each player is dealt one card
face down, followed by a second card face up. If anyone
is dealt the A♦ face up he takes all of the counters on the
table and the deal moves to the player on the dealer's
left.

If the A♦ is not turned up, each player in turn turns up his down card and wins the contents of the appropriate compartment if he has one of the following combinations:

MATRIMONY	**ANY KING AND QUEEN**
INTRIGUE	**ANY QUEEN AND JACK**
CONFEDERACY	**ANY KING AND JACK**
PAIR`	**TWO CARDS OF THE SAME RANK**
BEST	**HIGHEST DIAMOND**

Any stake not claimed goes forward to the next deal.

NAP

THREE TO SEVEN PLAYERS (FOUR OR FIVE IS BEST)

EACH PLAYER SHOULD HAVE A STOCK OF MATCHSTICKS, COUNTERS OR SIMILAR

The players are dealt five cards each, either singly or in batches of three and two. Beginning with the player on the dealer's left each takes it in turn to bid or pass. A bid involves saying that you will take a stated number of tricks with a suit of your choice as trumps. Bids rank as follows: two tricks, three, miz (misery or misère) (lose every trick), four, Nap (take all five tricks). Each player must either bid higher than the player before or pass.

The highest bidder leads the first trick. The suit of the card led determines trump for the hand, unless miz, which has no trumps, is being played. The winner of each trick takes the lead for the next. Players must follow suit if possible and the trick is won by the highest card of the suit led or the highest trump played. Ace ranks high.

If the bidder is successful he wins from each opponent two counters for a bid of two, three for a bid of three, four for four, three for miz or ten for nap. If he fails he pays the same amount to each opponent.

The pack is not usually reshuffled until a bid of nap has been won.

NEWMARKET

PACK OF 52 CARDS PLUS A♥ K♣ Q♦ J♠ FROM ANOTHER PACK AS 'PAY' OR 'BOODLE' CARDS

THREE TO EIGHT PLAYERS (FIVE IS BEST)

EACH PLAYER SHOULD HAVE A STOCK OF MATCHES, COUNTERS OR SIMILAR FOR BETTING

The pay cards are placed in the middle of the table. Before the deal each player places an agreed amount in a kitty in the middle and on the pay card of their choice. The dealer then deals out all the cards to each player and to an extra 'dummy' hand. It doesn't matter if some players have an extra card.

The dealer has the first option on taking the dummy hand instead of his own. If he does not want it, and provided that he hasn't looked at it, one of the other players may take it in exchange for an agreed payment to the kitty.

The player to the left of the dealer begins by putting down the lowest card in his hand of any suit he chooses. Cards rank from Ace to King. The player with the next highest card of the suit continues. Cards should be placed in front of the player, not in a general pile in the middle. If a player puts down a card that is the same as one of the pay cards he collects any counters that have been placed on it.

If a sequence comes to a stop (because the next card is in the dummy) a new sequence is started by the player of the last card. He does this by playing a card of a different colour to that last played. It must be the lowest card held in that colour. The first player to play the last card in his hand wins the kitty.

Alternative versions of the game use four Kings as pay cards. These may be taken from another pack or from the pack being used for play, in which case winnings are collected on playing the Queen of the relevant suit.

OH HELL!

THREE TO SEVEN PLAYERS (FOUR IS BEST)

The object of the game is to take the number of tricks you say you will!

One player should be appointed to keep score. Cut the cards to determine who deals, whoever draws the lowest card deals first.

One card is dealt to each player to begin. After examining his card, each player must make a bid. This is the number of tricks he will take, from 'none' or 'pass' to 'all'. For the first hand it is obviously one or pass. The bids should be noted down by the scorekeeper who announces whether the total bids are 'over', 'under' or 'even' the total number of tricks available.

The player to the dealer's left leads for the first trick. The trick is won by the highest card of the suit led and the winner leads for the next trick. Ace ranks high. There are no trumps in the first hand.

A player who succeeds in taking the exact number of tricks nominated wins 10 points plus the number of tricks taken. Players who fail to take the right number score nothing. The scorekeeper keeps note of everyone's score.

The deal passes to the left. The pack is reshuffled and two cards are dealt to each player. On each subsequent hand the number of cards dealt is increased by one until it is no longer possible to give each player the same number of cards. In a four-player game the last hand will be of thirteen cards. After the cards have been dealt the next card is turned up to determine trumps for the hand. The last hand is played without trumps.

The winner is the player with the highest score at the end of the last deal.

OLD MAID

PACK OF 52 CARDS (USE TWO PACKS IF MORE THAN SIX PLAY) WITH THE Q♥ REMOVED

THREE TO TEN PLAYERS

THIS GAME IS SUITABLE FOR YOUNG PLAYERS

The object is to avoid losing by being the one left with the 'Old Maid'.

All the cards are dealt out to the players. It doesn't matter if some have more than others. Each player sorts through his cards setting aside any pairs, for example two Aces, two 5s, two Jacks and so on. If he has three cards of the same rank in his hand only two can be set aside and the third must be kept in the hand.

After the players have sorted out their pairs the dealer fans out his remaining cards face down on the table. The player on his left takes one of the cards and adds it to his own hand. If this card completes a pair he puts them aside. The player then fans out his cards for the next player to make a selection.

The game continues in this way with each player in turn fanning out his cards for the next player to take one. At the end of the game every card will be paired off except for one of the Queens, which will have no pair. The person left holding this card, the 'Old Maid', is the loser.

PONTOON

THREE TO TEN PLAYERS

EACH PLAYER SHOULD HAVE A STOCK OF MATCHSTICKS, COUNTERS OR SIMILAR FOR BETTING

CARDS RANK AS FOLLOWS:
2 TO 10 COUNT THEIR PIP VALUE
COURT CARDS COUNT 10
ACES COUNT 1 OR 11 ACCORDING
TO THE PLAYER'S CHOICE

The dealer can be decided by cutting cards, the player cutting the highest card taking the deal. The dealer is also the banker. The aim of the players is to receive cards scoring more than the point value of the dealer's hand while avoiding going 'bust' by scoring over 21. A hand scoring 21 with two cards, i.e. an Ace plus a card worth 10, is a pontoon and pays extra.

The banker deals one card to each player and one to himself. The players examine their cards and may bet an amount on them up to an agreed maximum stake. The banker covers the bets then deals a second card face down to each player and one face up to himself. The banker does not look at his card. If any player has a pontoon he turns the Ace face up and makes no more bets.

The banker then asks each player in turn if he wants more cards. The player may elect to 'stick', that is take no more cards, providing his point total is at least 16. Alternatively, he may 'twist' and be given a card face up, or 'buy' a card, in which case he increases his stake and is dealt another card face down. He may not buy for more than his original stake but subsequent bets may be for less than the previous one.

The player may continue to twist or buy until he sticks or busts. No player may hold more than five cards (a five-card trick). If the player busts he loses his stake and hands his cards to the banker who places them at the bottom of the pack. If a player begins by twisting he may not subsequently buy in that deal, although if he begins by buying he may subsequently twist.

A player may not buy a fifth card if the total of the four cards already held adds up to 11 or less.

When all the players have finished the banker turns up his own cards and may add more cards to his hand until he is happy with his score or busts.

If the banker has a pontoon he wins all the stakes.
If the banker has 21 in three or more cards he pays double to any player holding a pontoon but wins all other stakes.
If the banker has under 21 he pays any player who has a higher count than he has (double for pontoon) and wins all other stakes.

If the banker busts he keeps the stakes of any players who have bust but pays everyone else.

If a player holds a five-card trick this beats everything except a pontoon held by the banker and is paid double.

If a player makes 21 with three 7s this beats everything except pontoon and he wins treble his original stake.

If a player has a pontoon and the bank does not the bank passes to that player.

EXAMPLE HAND

BANKER

PLAYER ONE

PLAYER TWO

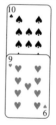

In this case the Banker pays Player One, who beats his 19 with a 20, but takes Player Two's stake because, although he also has 19, the Banker always wins a tied hand.

RANTER GO ROUND

THREE TO TEN PLAYERS

A GOOD GAME FOR YOUNG PLAYERS

The object of the game is to avoid losing a life by being the one holding the lowest card at the end of play. The cards rank from Ace (low) to King (high). Each player starts with three lives.

Players take it in turns to deal. Each gets one card face down. Beginning with the player on the dealer's left, each player in turn may either keep his card, which he turns face up if it is a King, or demand to exchange cards with the player on his left. The player on the left can only refuse to exchange if he holds a King, which he must show. The dealer may either keep his card or change it for another, which he cuts from the pack. The players then reveal their cards and the player with the lowest card loses a life.

ROLLING STONE

FOUR TO SIX PLAYERS

A GOOD GAME FOR YOUNG PLAYERS

Ideally there should be eight times as many cards as their are players, so for six players remove the 2s, for five players remove the 2s, 3s and 4s and for four players remove the 2s, 3s, 4s, 5s, and 6s.

The object is to be the first to run out of cards.

Deal eight cards to each player. The player on the dealer's left plays any card face up to the centre of the table. The other players must play cards of the same suit if possible. The highest card wins the trick and that player leads the next one. If a player cannot follow suit he must take all of the cards so far played and add them to his hand. He then leads the next trick.

The winner is the first player to play the last card from his hand.

RUMMY

PACK OF 52 CARDS (FIVE OR MORE PLAYERS MAY USE TWO PACKS SHUFFLED TOGETHER)

TWO TO TEN PLAYERS

PENCIL AND PAPER FOR KEEPING SCORE

The object of the game is to be the first to go out by collecting sequences of three or more cards in the same suit and in numerical order (Ace to King), or sets of three or more cards of the same rank. These are then laid face up on the table as 'melds'.

EXAMPLES OF MELDS

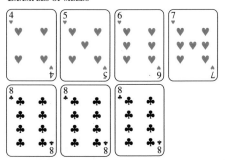

Decide who is to deal. The dealer deals seven cards to each player one at a time and an eighth card to himself. The remainder of the cards are placed on the table to form the stockpile. The dealer begins play by discarding one of the cards in his hand.

The next player can elect either to take the discard or to take the top card from the stockpile. If he has a meld he lays it down on the table in front of him. He then plays a card to the discard pile.

Play proceeds in this way with each player in turn drawing a card from the stockpile or the discard pile and then discarding a card. Once a player has succeeded in making an initial meld he can then play single cards from his hand by adding them to melds already placed on the table, either by himself or by an opponent. For example if the player holds 7♣ in his hand he may lay it off to;

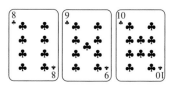

or three 7s.

The player may make as many melds and lay offs as possible before discarding and ending his turn.

Play ends when someone plays the last card in his hand, either as a meld, a lay off or a discard. That player then scores the value of the cards left in the other players hands, numerals counting at face value, court cards 10 and Aces 1. Alternatively players left with cards in their hands may count their value as a penalty score.

The game can continue until an agreed score has been reached.

SLAPJACK

**IF MORE THAN THREE PLAY TWO PACKS OF CARDS MAY BE
SHUFFLED TOGETHER**

THIS IS A GOOD GAME FOR YOUNG PLAYERS

The object of the game is to win all 52 cards.

All of the cards are dealt out to the players. It does not
matter if some have more cards than others. The players
should put their cards in a pile face down in front of
them without looking at them.

The player to the left of the dealer begins by putting a
card face up in the centre. The player to his left does the
same thing. Play continues with each player adding a card
one at a time to the pile in the centre until someone plays
a Jack. Every player then tries to be the first to 'slap the
Jack' by putting his hand on top of it. The player who
does so wins all of the cards in the central pile and puts
them at the bottom of his own pile. If two or more
players slap together the winner is the one with his hand
underneath the rest. The player to the winner's left starts
the next round.

Players shouldn't turn up their cards in such a way as to
get a peek at them before the others and turning and

slapping should be done with the same hand.

If a player runs out of cards he gets one last chance to stay in the game. He must wait until the next Jack is turned up and try to be the first to slap it. If he succeeds he wins the cards and can play on. If he doesn't he is out.

If a player slaps the wrong card he must give his next card, face down, to the player on his left.

SNAP

TWO OR MORE PLAYERS

THE CLASSIC CHILDREN'S CARD GAME – FAST, NOISY AND FUN!

Deal all the cards out to the players. It doesn't matter if some have more than others. Each player keeps his cards face down, either on the table or in his hand. In turn, each player plays his top card as quickly as possible into the centre of the table. When a card is played that is the same rank as the previous card the first player to shout 'Snap!' wins the pile of cards in the centre and adds them to the cards in his hand.

If one player snaps when the top two cards aren't the same, or if two players snap at the same time, the central pile is put to one side and a new pile is started. If a card is played to the new pile that matches the top card of the old pile the first player to call out 'Snap pool!' wins the old pile.

Another way to play is to have no central pile but for each player to keep their own upturned pile in front of them. Whenever a card is played that matches the top card on another pile the first player to call 'Snap!' wins both piles.

In both games the winner is the player who ends up with all 52 cards.

SNIP-SNAP-SNOREM!

THREE OR MORE PLAYERS

The object of the game is to get rid of all of your cards.

Cut the cards to decide who deals, Ace is high and highest card is dealer. Deal out all the cards face down to the players. It doesn't matter if some players have more than others.

The player on the dealer's left begins by placing any card face up on the table. The next player then plays a card of the same rank, if he has one, calling 'snip!' as he does so. If he does not have a card of matching rank he must pass and the player on his left takes a turn. The player who puts down the third card in the set calls out 'snap!' as he plays it. When the fourth and final card of the set is played the player calls out 'snorem!'.

If a player has more than one card of the rank asked for he may play them all together saying, 'snip snap!' if he has two, or 'snip-snap-snorem!' if he has three.

SNIP!

SNAP!

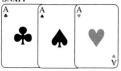

SNOREM!

SPIT!

TWO PLAYERS

The object is to get rid of all of your cards.

The cards are divided equally between the players. Each player then lays cards down in front of him as follows: starting from the left, three cards are placed face down in a row followed by a fourth card face up; from the left again, another face-down card is placed on the first two cards and a face-up card on the third; a face-down card is placed on the first pile and a face-up card on the second pile; finally, a face-up card is placed on the first pile.

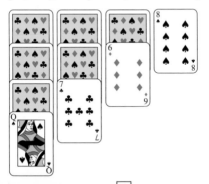

The players put their remaining cards in a pile, face down, beside this layout.

When both players are ready one shouts 'Spit!' Both players take the top card from their spare pile and place them face up together in the centre of the table.

Moving as quickly as possible, each player plays as many of his face-up cards as he can to his card in the centre. The cards must be played in sequence, either up or down. For example, if the centre card is 6, then a 7 or a 5 may be played to it. Suit is not important. When a player reveals one of the face-down cards in his layout he turns it face up.

Play continues until neither player can add a card to the centre. One player then shouts 'Spit!' and both put a card from their spare pile on to their pile in the centre. Play then continues. If neither player can play to the centre one shouts 'Spit!' again and another card is added to each player's central pile.

If a player's spare pile runs out he takes his central pile, turns it over, and uses that as a spare pile.

The first round ends when one player has played all of the cards from his layout on to his central pile. He shouts 'Out!' and picks up his spare pile. The other player picks up both central piles, his spare pile and any cards remaining in his layout.

Each player puts down another layout as before and play continues. After the first round, if a player runs out of cards in his spare pile he must play without it and both players add to the same central pile.

The winner is the first player to get rid of all his cards.

SWITCH

TWO TO TEN PLAYERS

**IF THERE ARE MORE THAN SIX IT MAY BE BEST TO SHUFFLE
TWO PACKS TOGETHER**

This game has many variations and this is just one
possible way to play it. The object is to get rid of all of
the cards in your hand.

Seven cards are dealt face down to each player. The
remainder are placed face down on the table as the
stockpile and the first card is turned face up

The player on the dealer's left goes first. He may play a
card of the same suit or rank as the upturned card. For
example, if the upturned card is 6♠ he has the choice of
playing another 6 or another spade. Alternatively he may
play any Ace. This entitles him to change the suit to one
of his choice – it need not be that of the Ace played.

If a player is unable to make any of the above plays he
must take a card from the stockpile into his hand and
play passes to the left. If the stockpile is used up before
the game is won the cards, with the exception of the last
one played, are gathered up and shuffled and put down
as a new stockpile.

If a 2 is played the next player must take two cards from

the stockpile unless he also has a 2, in which case the next player must take four cards. If the next player also has a 2 the next player will have to draw six cards ending with perhaps one unlucky player without a 2 drawing eight cards from the stockpile. Threes carry the same penalty with three, six, nine and twelve cards being drawn according to how many 3s are played in succession.

Playing a 7 reverses the direction of play. An 8 causes the next person to miss a turn.

Play continues until one player plays his last card. A player with two cards left must announce 'Last card' on playing one of them. If he fails to do so he must take a card from the stockpile.

THIRTY-ONE

THREE TO TEN PLAYERS (FIVE OR MORE IS BEST)

EACH PLAYER SHOULD HAVE A STOCK OF MATCHSTICKS, COUNTERS OR SIMILAR

The object of the game is to have, in descending order, three cards of the same suit totalling 31, three cards of the same rank, or the highest total in any one suit. For scoring, Aces count 11 points, number cards their pip value and court cards 10 points.

Before the deal each player puts an agreed number of counters into the kitty. Three cards are dealt to each player and three face up into the centre as the 'widow'.

The player on the dealer's left begins by drawing one card from the widow and discarding one from his hand. Each player in turn does the same. No player may take more than one card and no player may pass. Play continues until one player announces that he has 31 points, shows his cards and wins the kitty.

At any time during play a player may rap the table if he thinks his current hand is good enough to win after he has drawn and discarded. The other players may, in their turn, choose to stand or to exchange one more card with the widow. All players then show their hands and the highest score wins.

The player only needs to exchange his 7♦ for the Q♥ in the widow for a winning hand of 31.

TUNK

TWO TO FIVE PLAYERS

**IF THERE ARE FOUR OR FIVE PLAYERS USE TWO PACKS OF
CARDS SHUFFLED TOGETHER**

The rules of the game are similar to those of Rummy.
The object is to collect sequences of three or more cards
in the same suit and in numerical order (Ace to King), or
sets of three or more cards of the same rank. In this game
twos are wild cards, which means they can be used to
stand for any other rank in a meld.

Each player is dealt seven cards and the top card is
turned over as the starter. Beginning with the player on
the dealer's left, play proceeds round the table with each
player trying to build up sets in his hand. As soon as a set
is completed the player places it face up on the table in
front of him. The player may subsequently add to his
meld if able to do so. Unlike Rummy, however, players
may not add to each other's melds. A player can go out
as long as he has reduced the total of the unmatched
cards in his hand to five or less (Aces count as one).

Before a player goes out he must announce that he is
about to do so by saying 'Tunk' when it is his turn. That
is all the player may do in that turn. The other players
then have one last turn to try to reduce the total of the
unmelded cards in their hands. The player who called

Tunk then lays down his cards when it gets back to his turn. The other players may, if they are able, add cards from their hands to the tunker's melds.

The tunker's score is zero and all the other players add up the point score of all the unmelded cards in their hands. A record is kept of the scores and when a player reaches 100 points he is out of the game. Play continues untill there is just one player left.

VATICAN

TWO TO FIVE PLAYERS (THREE OR FOUR IS BEST)

TWO PACKS OF 52 CARDS PLUS JOKERS

Rather like Rummy, the object of the game is to be the first to go out by laying all of one's cards on the table in sets.

After the cards are shuffled the player on the dealer's left cuts the cards. If he cuts a Joker he may keep it and is subsequently dealt twelve more cards. Thirteen cards are dealt to each player and the rest are placed face down on the table as the stockpile.

In turn, each player takes a card from the stockpile and adds it to his hand. He does not discard any cards but may, if possible, play a suit sequence of three or more cards face up on the table in front of him. Ace may count high or low but not both at the same time, so King Ace Two is not allowed.

When a player has made an initial meld his options increase on subsequent turns. He may make another meld but this time sets of three or four cards of the same rank are allowed as well as sequences. He can add cards to any melds placed on the table, either by himself or by one of the other players.

A player may also rearrange melds on the table, moving cards from one to another and adding cards from his own hand. However, he may only do so if at the end of his rearranging all the cards on the table still form valid melds of three or more cards and he adds at least one card from his hand.

A Joker may be played to represent any other card. Players may subsequently substitute the card it represents for the Joker, which may then be moved to another meld.

The first player to put all his cards on the table wins the game.

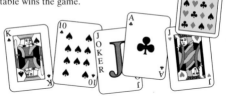

WAR

TWO PLAYERS

The object is to win all of the cards.

The whole pack is dealt out between the two players.
Both players place their cards face down in a pile in front
of them without looking at them.

Each player takes the top card of his pile and places it
face up in the middle of the table. The player whose
cards has the higher rank (suit is irrelevant) wins both
cards and adds them to the bottom of his pile. Play continues in this way with players collecting cards.

When two cards of the same rank are
turned over war breaks out. Both players
then put one card face down on top of
their first card, followed by a third card
face up. The highest ranking of the last
pair of cards played wins all six cards. If
these cards are also of the same rank
the war continues, with each player
putting down two more cards, one
face down, one face up, until someone
wins.

The game ends when one player has all
the cards.

A WAR

PLAYER ONE

PLAYER TWO

Player One wins!

PATIENCE GAMES

A patience, or solitaire, game is generally speaking one that is played by a single player (although see Spite and Malice for an example of a two-player patience).

The object of all patience games is to get the cards into a certain order, usually with the suits separated and in rank order, beginning from an initial layout of some or all of the cards. The starting layout is the distinguishing feature of most patience games.

Games differ in the degrees of skill involved and as with any card game chance plays a big part in determining whether or not a game will 'come out'. Some, such as The Wish, depend purely on luck in the way that the cards fall in the initial deal, whereas others, such as Grandma's Game, can involve a certain amount of calculation and skill.

There may well be more patience games than there are any other type of card games and the following is just a small sample of the many that exist.

ACES HIGH

THIS IS A FAIRLY SIMPLE GAME THAT IS SUITABLE FOR CHILDREN

Shuffle the pack and deal four cards, face up, in a row to form four tableaus. If two or more of those cards have the same suit, move the lower-ranked ones on to a discard pile.

When you can make no more moves, deal four more cards on to the tableaus, placed so that you can see the cards underneath.

Only the topmost card of each tableau is available. Continue to move cards to the discard pile if they match the suit of any higher-ranked available card. If a pile is emptied, you must fill it with any available card from another tableau before you can deal again.

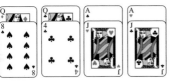

In the example shown the 4♣ may be discarded (because it is lower than the J♣), then the J♣ (because it is lower than the Q♣ that has been exposed) then the J♥ (because the A♥ has been revealed) and finally the 8♠ when the A♠ is uncovered.

Because Aces are high, they cannot be discarded. The goal is to complete the game with all other cards discarded, and the Aces laid out, one in each tableau.

CANFIELD

SOME THOUGHT IS REQUIRED IN PLAYING THIS GAME AND WINS ARE RARE

The layout has a row of four foundations with four piles below them. Keep the stockpile to the left of the layout and form the discard pile to the right. Deal thirteen cards face down into the stockpile, then turn the whole stockpile over so that it is face-up but with only the top card visible. Deal one card face-up on to each pile. Deal one card face-up on to the first foundation. Keep the rest of the pack in your hand.

The foundations are built up in suit order. The rank of the card dealt on to the first foundation determines the starting rank for all the foundations. The other foundation piles must be started with a card that matches the rank of the card placed on the first foundation in the initial layout. (For example, in the layout shown overleaf the first card placed on a foundation pile is a Jack so the other foundations will begin with a Jack as well.) Building is circular, with Ace following King.

The piles beneath the foundations may be built down in alternating colour so that, for example a red 8 is played on to a black 9. Again building is circular, with King following Ace.

The top cards of both the stockpile and the wastepile are

available for building on either the piles or the foundations and the top cards of the piles are available for building on the foundations. Full builds in the piles may be moved on to other piles; partial builds may not be moved.

JACK   JACK   JACK

STOCKPILE

WASTEPILE

Empty piles must be filled immediately with the top card of the stockpile. If the stockpile is empty, you may use the top card of the wastepile, but in this case, you need not fill empty piles until you are ready.

You may deal from the cards in your hand at any time, by turning a three-card packet face up on to the wastepile. You may redeal as often as you wish. When you have played out all the cards in your hand you may pick up the wastepile and start again.

GOLF

AN UNUSUAL SCORING SYSTEM, WHERE LOWER SCORES ARE BETTER THAN HIGHER ONES, GIVES THIS GAME ITS NAME

Lay out seven columns, each with five face-up cards, as shown in the example. Place a single face-up card to start the discard pile. Keep the rest of the pack in your hand.

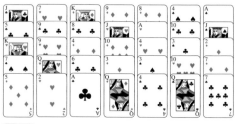

DISCARD PILE

The object of the game is to move as many cards as possible from the layout into the discard pile. The top cards in each column are available for building on to the discard pile, either up or down by rank – suit and colour do not matter. Nothing may be built on a King and cards may not be moved from one column to another.

Play by turning up a single card from your hand when you can no longer play from the layout.

In the example several options available. The 7♣ may be played on to the 6♥, but it would be better to play the 5♦ followed by the 4♣, 3♠, 2♥ and A♣.

Because this is a hard game to win, many people 'play for par'. Think of each game as a 'hole', and the number of cards left in the layout at the end as the number of 'strokes' you took to play the hole. Each hole is par 4, so par for nine holes, or games, is 36.

GRANDPA'S CLOCK

Separate the following cards from the deck, and lay them out in a circle like the numbers on a clock face, starting at 1 o'clock and carrying on clockwise around the face to 12 o'clock: 10♥, J♠, Q♦, K♣, 2♥, 3♠, 4♦, 5♣, 6♥, 7♠, 8♦, 9♣. These twelve cards form the foundations. Shuffle the remaining cards and lay them out in eight columns of five cards each, face up and fanned down as shown below.

The first card of each column is available for play. Columns can be built down, regardless of suit or colour. Empty columns may be filled with any available card. Foundations build up in suit. Building is circular: on columns, a King may be played on an Ace, while on foundations an Ace may be played on a King.

The goal is to build each foundation up to its appropriate number on the clock face. (This means that the foundations at 1, 2, 3, and 4 o'clock will finish with five cards each, while the rest will finish with four.)

In the example layout shown the 7♥ and 8♥ may be moved to the 6♥ at the 9 o'clock position, the 5♥ can be moved to the 4♦ at 7 o'clock and the 3♥ may be moved on to the 2♥ at 5 o'clock, and so on.

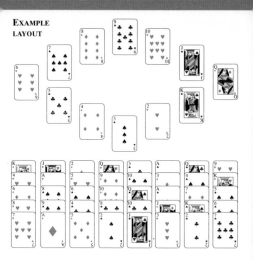

The game is won when the clock face is in the correct number order from one to twelve with the Ace at 1 o'clock and the Jack and Queen at 11 o'clock and 12 o'clock.

GRANDMA'S GAME

THIS GAME WILL REWARD THOUGHT AND PLANNING WITH FREQUENT WINS

Shuffle two full packs of cards together. You will need to deal out 13 piles in whatever arrangement is most convenient for the surface area you have to play on. The first pile is the 'Ace' pile, the second is the '2' pile, and so on up to the 13th pile, which is the 'King' pile. There are also eight foundation piles, which are empty at the start.

Begin by dealing one card on to the Ace pile, then one on to the 2 pile, and so on up to the King pile. Then start with the Ace pile again and continue until all the cards have been dealt. Keep the piles neat so that you can see only the topmost card of each. It's all part of the game to try and remember where some of the cards are hidden.

Whenever you deal a King put the next card aside face down in a stockpile; whenever you deal a card on to the 5 pile, the 10 pile, or the King pile put the next card face down into the stockpile; and whenever the card's rank matches that of the pile it is dealt to, for example if you deal 7♦ on to the 7 pile, again deal the next card face down into the stockpile.

If you deal a 5 on to the 5 pile you have to deal two cards to the stockpile, one because it is the 5 pile and one because the 5's rank matches its pile's rank If you deal a

King on to the King pile, you would have to deal three cards face down into the stockpile: one for the King, one for the King pile, and one for the matching ranks.

The stockpile will probably end up with 20 to 30 cards in it. The piles will usually contain five or six cards.

The top cards of the piles and the foundations, when they are started are available for building on to the foundations. There are two foundations for each suit, one should start with an Ace and build up in suit to the King; the other should start with a King and build down in suit to the Ace.

When you have made all the moves possible using the face-up cards at the start, deal one card from the stockpile face-up on to the pile that matches its rank. For example, if you deal a 7 you would place it on top of the 7 pile. Pick up the entire pile and fan it out. All of the cards in the pile are now available for moving on to foundations, in addition to the top cards of the piles. You are also allowed to change the order of the cards in the fanned-out pile. The challenge is to try to predict which cards you will need first and which you won't and move them to the top or bottom of the fan so that when you return the cards to the correct pile they will be in the best order to win the game.

Since there are two foundation piles for each suit, one building up and one down, there will be times when, for example, the 'down' pile may be showing the 6, while the 'up' pile is showing the 5. If something like this happens, you may move the 6 (and other cards) from the 'down' to the 'up' pile if that helps move a card from a layout pile to a foundation.

The goal is to move all cards to the foundations.

EXAMPLE LAYOUT

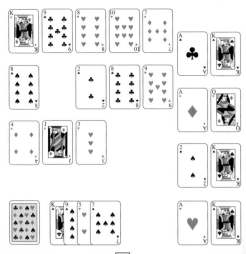

KLONDIKE

Deal out a row of one face-up and six face-down cards. Deal another card face up on the first face-down card and then a face-down card on the next five cards. Deal a face-up card on the first face-down column and a face-down card on the rest. Carry on in this way until you have a layout like the one shown with seven cards in the last column.

The aim is to build up all of the cards in suit order, beginning with the Aces. When an Ace becomes available it should be put at the top of the layout as a foundation.

Turn up cards one at a time from the pack and if possible play them to the layout. Cards on the layout build down in rank order and alternating colours. For example, a red 7 can only be played on a black 8. Alternatively, a card may be played to a foundation if it is next up in suit sequence. If neither of these things can be done the card is placed face up on a wastepile. The top card of the wastepile may be played any time it is possible to do so.

The face-up cards on the layout are also available for play and may be built on each other. For instance, in the example layout the 9♥ and 8♠ may be moved on to the 10♣ and the A♥ can be moved up to start a foundation.

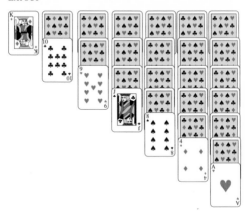

When two or more cards are built on each other they may only be moved as a unit so, for example, if you have a black 8, red 7 and black 6 together all three cards have to be moved together (on to a red 9). When a face-up card is moved from a column the face-down card beneath it is turned up.

If a column is emptied the space can be filled by a King.

Continue to turn over the cards from the stockpile one at a time, playing them to the layout when possible. You may only go through the stockpile once.

A variation, which has more chance of coming out, is to take cards from the stockpile in packs of three. The second and third cards only become available if you are able to play the cards that come before them.
You may go through the stockpile as many times as you wish.

THE WISH

THIS IS A VERY SIMPLE GAME AND IS SUITABLE FOR CHILDREN. YOU CAN MAKE A WISH WHEN YOU WIN A GAME!

Remove all the 2s, 3s, 4s, 5s, and 6s from the pack and discard them. Shuffle the remaining cards and deal them out in eight piles of four cards each, face up and squared off so only the top card shows.

Pairs of cards that match in rank (such as two 7s or two Kings) may be discarded. For example, in the layout shown the 9s, Kings and Aces can all be removed.

The goal is to discard all 32 cards.

SPITE AND MALICE

Two packs of cards are used. Pack A is a standard 52-card pack. Pack B should include four Jokers. The cards are ranked from King (high) to Ace (low).

Pack A is shuffled and divided into two piles of 26 cards each. These are the payoff piles and it is each player's task to get rid of his payoff pile. The players turn up the top cards of their payoff piles and the one who turns up the highest card will begin.

The second player shuffles Pack B and deals five cards face down to each player. Pack B is then placed in the centre of the table as the stockpile.

Any Aces available, whether from payoff piles or in the players' hands must be played immediately to the table to form centre piles. Both players can play cards to the centre piles, either from their payoff piles or from their hands. When the top card of the payoff pile is played to the centre the next card in the pile is turned face up. The centre piles are built up in rank order without regard to suit. When a centre stack has been built up to the King it is removed and shuffled back into the stockpile.

Each player is allowed four discard piles. A discard pile may be started with any card held in the hand and they are used when no play is possible to the centre piles. The discard piles can be added to by building down in rank (Jack on Queen, for example) or by cards of the same rank (a 4 on a 4). Cards from the discard piles may subsequently be played to the centre piles if it is possible to do so. It is not permitted to move cards between the discard piles.

In his turn a player may make as many plays to the centre piles as it is possible for him to do. The aim is to get rid of the top card in the payoff pile while at the same time avoiding plays that may open up opportunities for the opponent. A player's turn ends as soon as he plays a card to a discard pile. Only one card may be discarded in each turn. At the start of his next turn the player takes as many cards as are necessary from the stockpile to restore the number of cards in his hand to five.

Jokers are wild cards and may be played in place of any others except Aces.

The winner is the first player to get rid of all the cards in his payoff pile by playing them to the centre piles. It is no necessary to get rid of the cards held in hand in order to win.

GLOSSARY

Available card: in patience games any card that may be transferred from one place to another in the layout.

Bust: in Pontoon to have drawn cards totalling over 21 points.

Court cards: also called face cards, the King, Queen and Jack.

Crib: in Cribbage the extra hand that is formed from the players' discards.

Cut: to split the pack and show the card uncovered to determine who deals. Can also mean splitting the pack and placing the top half beneath the bottom half so that no one knows what the bottom card is.

Deadwood: in Rummy the unmatched cards remaining in your hand.

Deal: to hand out cards to the players at the start of a game.

Discard: to put aside an unwanted card.

Discard pile: the cards that have been put aside during a game.

Draw: to take one or more cards from a stockpile or wastepile.

Flush: cards that are all the same suit.

Foundation: in patience games a card on which a sequence must be built.

Gin: in Gin Rummy a hand that has no deadwood.

Go out: to play one's last card.

Hand: the cards dealt to a player at the start of the game.

Layout: in patience games the pattern of cards as first dealt out.

Lead: to play the first card in a trick.

Meld: a set of three or more cards matched in sequence according to suit or in sets of the same rank.

Pair: two cards of the same rank.

Pips: the suit marks or spots printed in the centre of a card.

Prial (or pair royal): three cards of the same rank.

Rank: the value of a card (Ace, 2, 3 … Jack, Queen, King).

Run: a sequence in rank order of three or more cards.

Stockpile: cards that are not dealt at the start but which may be used later in play.

Suit: Hearts, Clubs, Diamonds or Spades.

Trick: a round of cards played during the course of the game, won by the player who plays the highest ranking card.

Trump suit: a suit that out ranks the others, any card from the trump suit will beat any card from another suit.

Wild card: a card that may represent any other card.